# JAZZ CLASSICS
## FOR VIBRAPHONE

ARRANGED BY TIM McMAHON

ISBN 978-1-4950-9560-3

# Hal•LEONARD®

7777 W. BLUEMOUND RD. P.O. BOX 13819 MILWAUKEE, WI 53213

Visit Hal Leonard Online at
**www.halleonard.com**

This book is dedicated to all my students—past, present,
and future—who, through their efforts to progress and succeed,
have made me a better teacher, performer, and person.

# CONTENTS

# ACKNOWLEDGMENTS

I'd like to thank several masterful musicians for their suggestions and thoughts during the development of this book: Jazz bassist (and master woodworker) David Marr, pianist John Opferkuch, vibist/pianist Anthony Smith, and Jane Zwerneman for her assistance with music software

# ABOUT THE ARRANGER

Originally from Chicago, IL, Tim McMahon moved to southerm California in 1977 to finish high school. He began attending San Diego State University in 1981 and studied percussion with Danlee Mitchell. During his years at SDSU, he had many opportunities to study with other notable drummer/percussionists, and to study jazz piano and composition around the Southern California area as well. These inspiring teachers included Jon Szanto, Duncan Moore, David Garibaldi, Michael Spiro, Tim Shea, Billy Mintz, Charles McPherson, Jim Plank, Hal Crook, and, some years later, Richard Wilson and Rick Helzer. He graduated in 1986 as Outstanding Music Graduate of that year, and for a number of years, served as adjunct professor in the percussion department.

During and after his college years, Tim performed in San Diego and Los Angeles with many of the great jazz players of the day as well as with the San Diego Symphony Orchestra and San Diego Chamber Orchestra. He also did film/session work and theatre work. He was a member of guitarist Ron Eschete's trio performing in Los Angeles and along the West Coast. Other artists Tim has performed with over the years include alto saxophonist Charles McPherson, Art Farmer, Hank Jones, and Hollis Gentry.

As a drummer, he has several recordings available, including *Illuminations* (HeavyWood Music), which features trio, quartet, quintet, and sextet settings performing original compositions and arrangements.

At the present time, Tim keeps a busy schedule freelancing in the Southern California area and teaching.

For more information visit www.timdrums.com

# INTRODUCTION

This volume is the companion book to *Jazz Standards for Vibraphone* (HL06620168) and is a continuation of four-mallet arrangements for some of the great classic jazz tunes of our time. I simplified these arrangements technically, to some extent, and reduced the amount of "information" on the page. Indications like mallet numbering and dampening are kept to a minimum to provide a slightly cleaner page. The idea is that intermediate and advanced players will make those decisions easily and have a slightly less "busy" page to negotiate.

The standard chord changes are included to help with harmonic analysis. Reharmonization was kept to a minimum to aid in memorization. I recommend taking some time to decipher the voicings with the chord symbols to explore some other possibilities. Likewise, the melodies are written in their original form with very little alteration, with the occasional exception. The intention here is to learn the tune in its entirety and close to the composer's original idea; however, you should always feel free to make those melodies your own and dress them up to suit your own personal expression.

These arrangements were developed using the Burton grip. The mallets are numbered from left to right: "4, 3" in the left hand, and "2, 1" in the right. Some stickings are indicated as well as pedaling and dampening. Again, I kept the numbering to a minimum to avoid clutter on the page in addition to being mindful that players may use different grips.

Mallet dampening is indicated by an "x" after the note to be dampened, leading to the next note. Dampening and pedaling are, of course, left to the interpretation of the performer. Pedal gradations and mallet dampening should be explored to produce the essential melody notes while retaining control of the ability to change the undercurrent of harmonies. Much of this will be obvious since most arrangements contain the original melody as it would appear on a lead sheet.

No metronome markings are included in this volume as players will decide what is the right tempo for their goals.

I suggest both listening to recordings of the great jazz masters playing these classics, and memorizing the arrangements. I have found that memorizing tunes and changes is invaluable for freeing up the creative juices of improvisation and interpretation, especially in a jazz setting.

These arrangements will require some dedicated practice. They require some technical prowess and, in turn, will develop it. My hope is that you will benefit greatly from working on these pieces. Enjoy them!

Tim McMahon
San Diego, CA
August, 2017

# PERFORMANCE NOTES

### AUTUMN IN NEW YORK

This is the great Vernon Duke ballad and one of the more "notey" arrangements in this volume. Definitely take your time with it. It can ebb and flow. Sticking and dampening are indicated where they may be helpful. At m. 29, watch the pedal accuracy for clarity of the chord-melody line.

### FOOTPRINTS

The intro ostinato can be played with the indicated sticking to work the left hand, or it can be played with malleting 1,3,1,1. The malleting indicted at m. 9 can be employed throughout whenever there is a melody on top. Note at m. 29 the E-flat inner voice descends with mallet dampening as the pedal remains depressed for all four bars.

### GOODBYE PORK PIE HAT

In this classic Mingus tune, the arrangement has some really close-knit harmonies over the 7th chords. Take special note of m. 7 regarding this. A slow to medium tempo is good to let those darker voicings come out.

### I GOT RHYTHM

This is the classic song from which "Rhythm" changes were borrowed to create so many jazz classics. These tunes are commonly played rather briskly at sessions and performances. Because of this, the arrangement will lend itself (after some time in the "woodshed") to be played with some velocity.

It may take a bit of time to get the hand separation and pedaling in sync to express the tune clearly. Practice slowly and accurately.

### LULLABYE OF BIRDLAND

This great tune offers a few challenges. Note that the right-hand double stops at the very beginning occasionally change intervallically. Most of the single-note melody should be played with the number 1 mallet for smoothness. A medium swing tempo can be the goal here. Practice slowly and accurately before speeding up the tempo.

### NIGHT AND DAY

In this great Cole Porter tune (which is usually played by jazz musicians in C or E-flat), there are a few challenges for the vibraphonist. Because of some of the long melody notes, pedaling and dampening should be practiced to minimize blurriness. I've included some dampening, and the player should feel free to add more mallet dampening as needed. I've also included some mallet choice numbering. The chord changes are the standard harmony commonly used and not at all reharmonized.

### (THERE IS) NO GREATER LOVE

This tune is frequently called on sessions and gigs. In bars 17, 19, and 21 make sure the pedaling and note accuracy is right—it will bring out the chord melody quarter notes. This is a great selection to work on for speed.

## NUAGES

This is the classic Django Reinhardt tune. I used renowned guitarist Ron Eschete's chart to arrange it for vibraphone. I had (and still have) the great pleasure of working with Ron from time to time in his guitar trio, and also in an organ trio setting. We play this as a samba, but it can be played in many styles and as a ballad as well. The sticking in the pick-up bar at the very beginning is helpful throughout where the half-step melody movement is present. The dampening should be executed with same-mallet dampening. Measure 13 into 14 is tricky, but with the sticking indicated is pretty easily played. Note Ron's beautiful polychords in the coda. Take a little time through this section and let these harmonies speak.

## ON GREEN DOLPHIN STREET

The challenge here is the intertwining ostinato and melody play. The goal is to keep the bass line (which is typical for this tune) slightly lower in volume, and to bring out the melody. Closely observe the pedaling in the intro to get the flavor and punctuation of the groove. This song goes from a straight-eighth Latin feel to a swing feel for the second eight bars of A and B.

## SATIN DOLL

In this popular Duke Ellington tune, the famous intro is included and works nicely on the vibraphone. Starting at m. 13, the close-knit voicing movement can be tricky to keep smooth and swinging, especially at m. 15. Use the ends of the bars wherever possible. Don't forget to chime in vocally with "switch-a-rooney" at bar 28!

## SIDEWINDER

This is Lee Morgan's straight-eighth classic. The pedal is used somewhat sparingly to give the arrangement a more dry, punchy feeling. Most of the octave lines can be played with 1,3 mallets. The right-hand double stops can be played on the ends of the bars for ease in switching chords. In mm. 11–12, mallet 1 can play the full line alone while switching chords in the left hand.

## SOFTLY AS IN A MORNING SUNRISE

This is a favorite tune players love to call on gigs! There are a couple quick moves from bar 7 to 8 and then to bar 9. The sticking indicated will help that. Other than a few sticking challenges, this arrangement is pretty straightforward.

## STAR EYES

The well-known intro riff can be played with the right hand by itself or with mallets 1 and 3. The song has Latin and swing style sections. In performances on gigs, I've found that the whole form usually swings during solos, forgoing the back and forth, until the head is played again after improvisation.

At m. 9 the E-flat/B-flat in the melody on beat 1 can be dampened on the very edge of the bars with the right hand while playing the D-flat/A-flat with the left. This way the pedal can sustain throughout the bar and keep blurriness to a minimum. At mm. 22 and 24 the underlying melodic line is just a response to the previous measures respectively and not part of the actual line of the tune.

## STOLEN MOMENTS

The melody starting at m. 5 can be played as indicated with the 1 and 3 mallets, or with the right hand with occasional help from the number 3 mallet. At m. 13 it makes sense to play the eighth-note melody with the number 1 mallet to catch all the supporting harmonies smoothly.

## SUMMERTIME

This popular Gershwin gem is arranged to be played rather slowly and in a languid style, giving the moving lines time to "breathe." Melody lines at mm. 6 and 13 can be played with the right hand. At mm. 7 and 8, it's a bit easier to play the underlying line with the inner mallets.

## TAKE FIVE

Start out playing this one slow and swinging before picking up the pace. In the measures where there are sixteenth-note lines going to a chord (e.g., mm. 3 and 4), I've included some sticking that works well but will still require some practice to get the movement smooth. Measure 18 offers a bit more of a challenge because of the double stops. Slow, precise, and relaxed execution in your practice is key here. The descending quarter-note triplet at m. 23 can be played with the left hand.

## WALTZ FOR DEBBY

This is Bill Evans' classic 3/4 waltz that featured the great jazz bassist Scott LeFaro. There is a lot of interesting bass movement that really is the signature element of this beautiful tune. In this arrangement, I wanted to highlight that movement on the vibes, which makes for some very colorful harmony and works well on the vibraphone.

There are mostly dotted half-note chords and the melody, with a few exceptions. Generally, there are several chords that are orchestrated with large intervals, which may require a bit of attention for performance accuracy. Note at mm. 5 and 6 there is a mallet dampen from the C♯ to the C while pedaling through both measures. Use #2 mallet to do this, and the melody can be uninterrupted and sustained properly for those two bars. Use the same idea at mm. 21–22 and mm. 53–54.

# Footprints

By Wayne Shorter

# Autumn in New York

Words and Music by
Vernon Duke

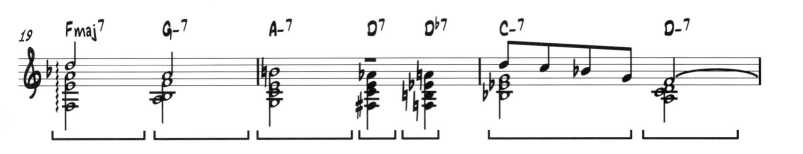

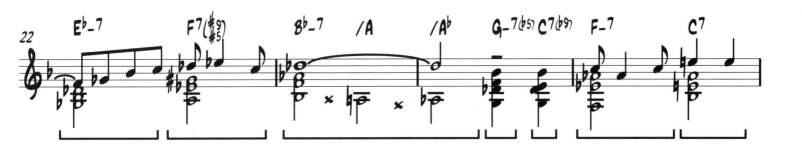

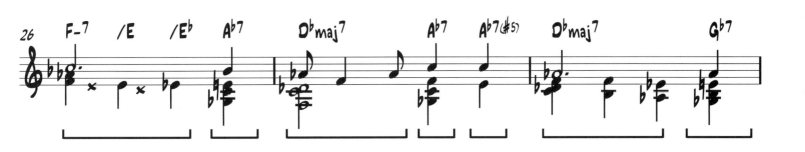

# I Got Rhythm
## FROM AN AMERICAN IN PARIS

Music and Lyrics by George Gershwin
and Ira Gershwin

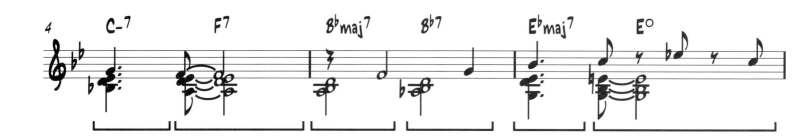

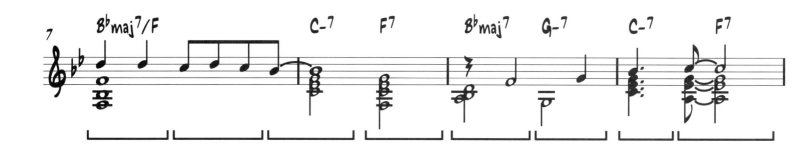

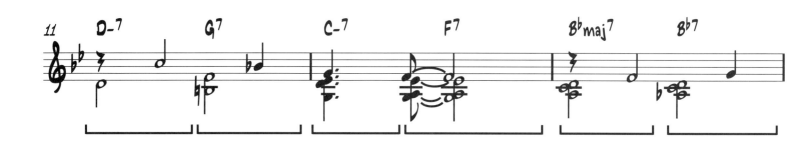

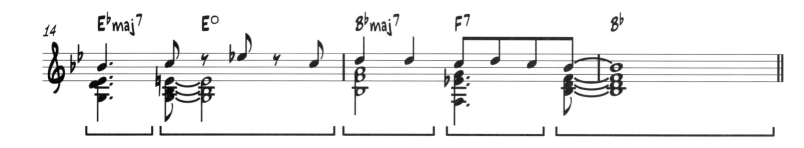

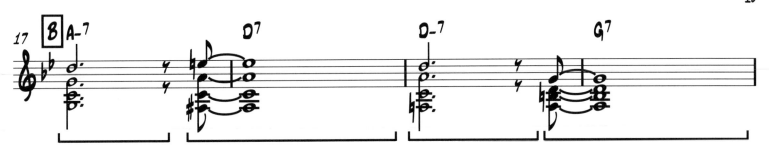

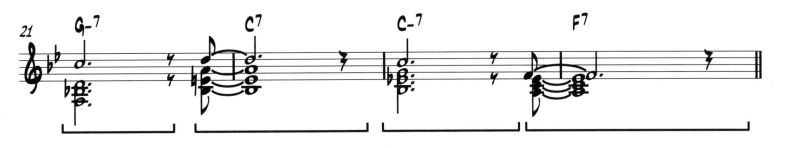

# Lullaby of Birdland

Words by George David Weiss
Music by George Shearing

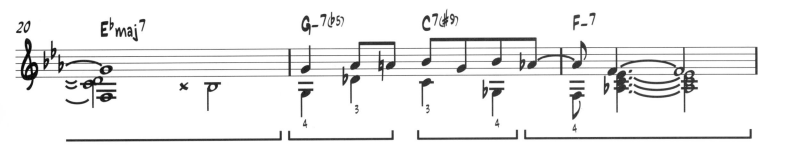

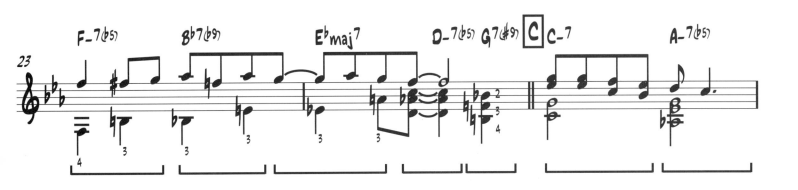

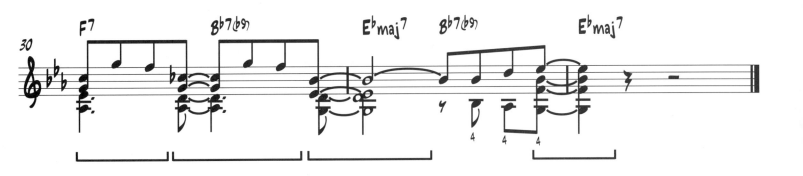

# Night and Day

FROM GAY DIVORCE
FROM THE GAY DIVORCEE

WORDS AND MUSIC BY
COLE PORTER

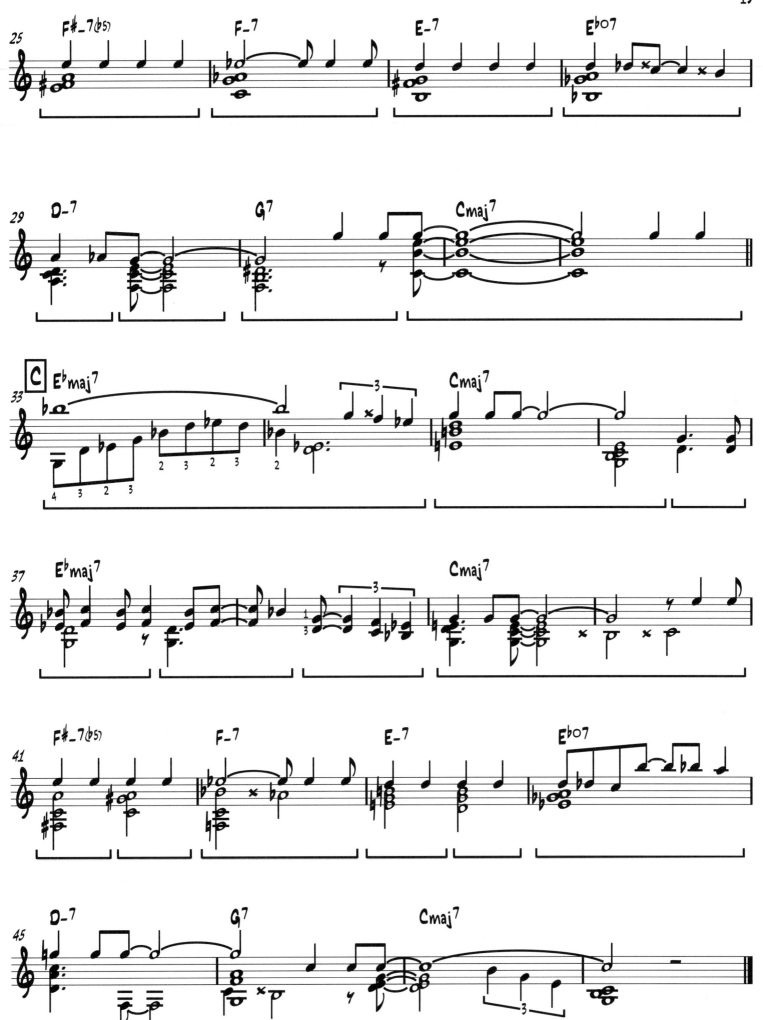

# (There Is)
# No Greater Love

Words by Marty Symes
Music by Isham Jones

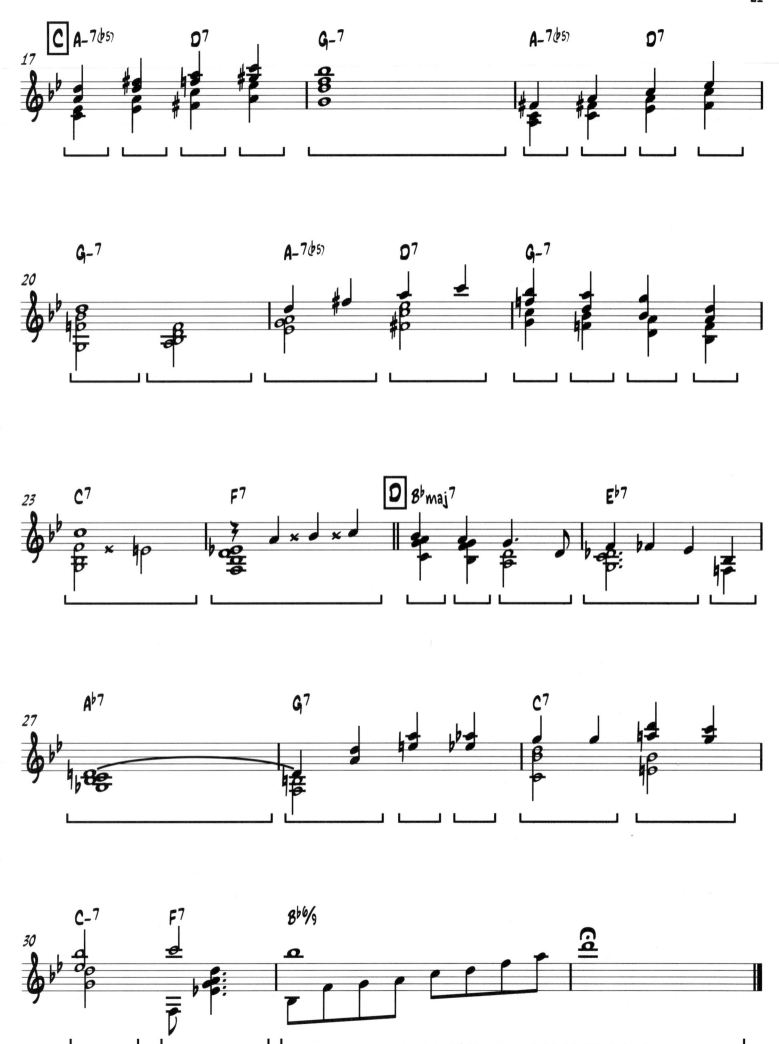

# Nuages

By Django Reinhardt
and Jacques Larue
(Lead sheet and changes
from Guitarist Ron Eschete)

# On Green Dolphin Street

Lyrics by Ned Washington
Music by Bronislau Kaper

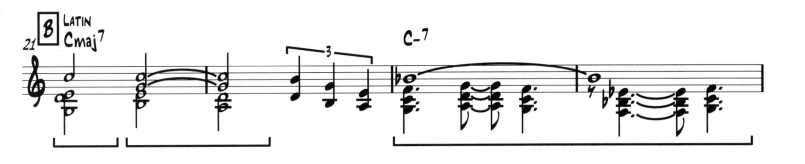

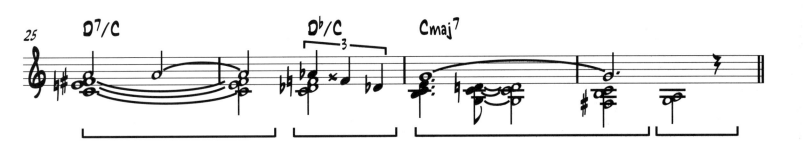

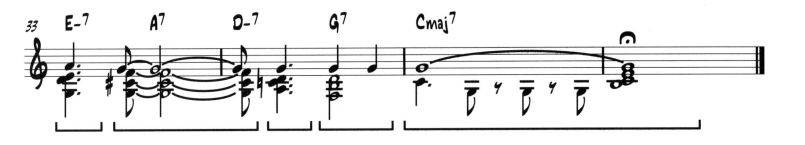

# Satin Doll

By Duke Ellington

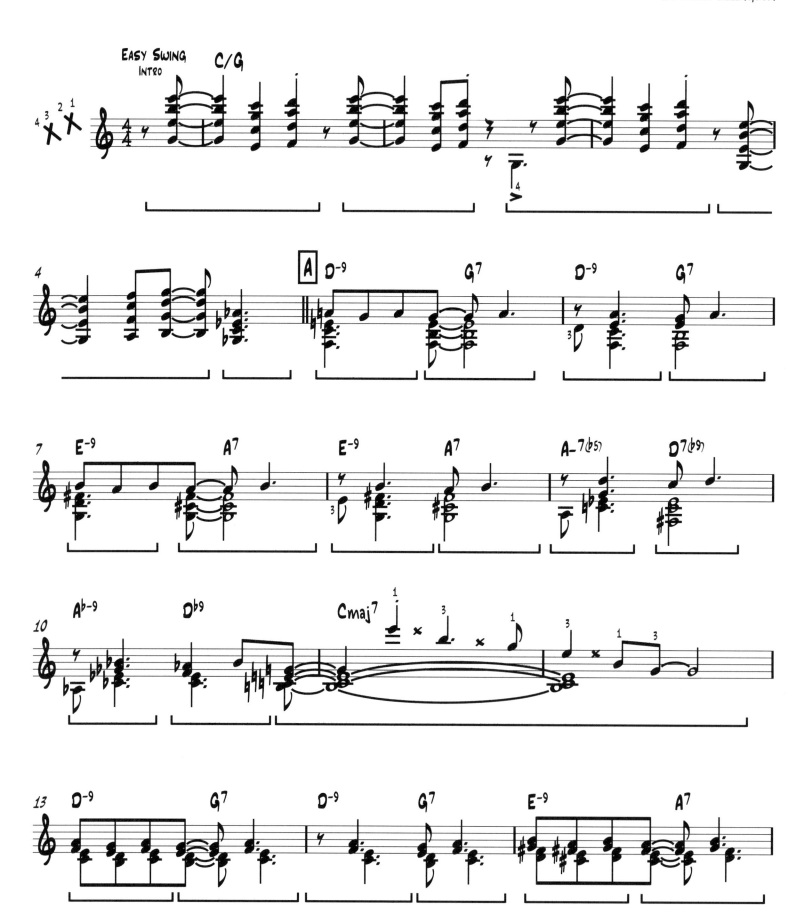

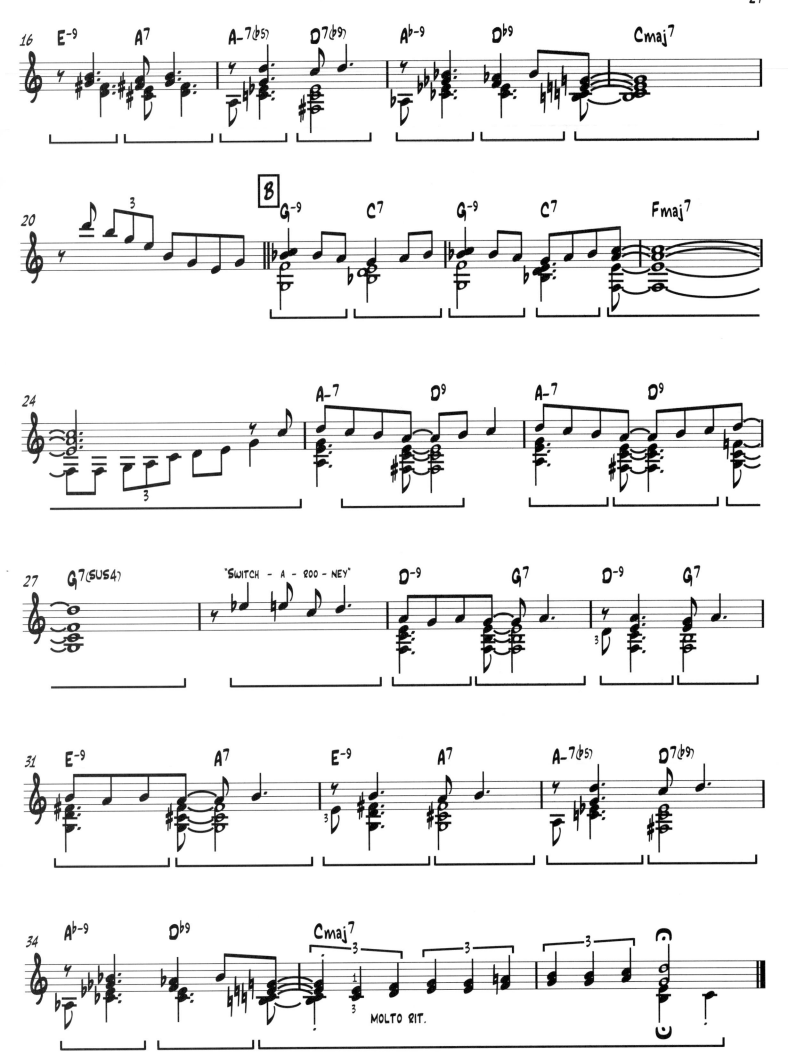

# Goodbye Pork Pie Hat

By Charles Mingus

Slow-swinging Jazz feel

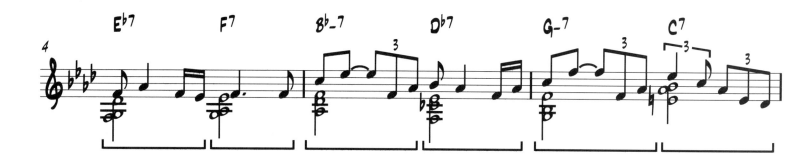

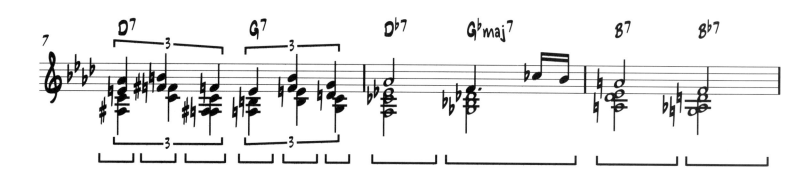

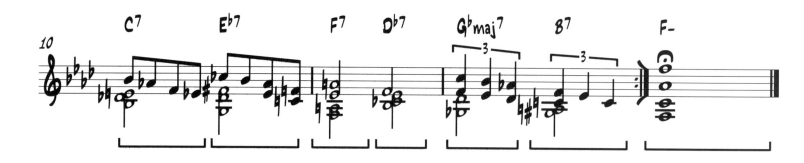

# Sidewinder

By Lee Morgan

# Softly As in a Morning Sunrise
FROM THE NEW MOON

Lyrics by Oscar Hammerstein II
Music by Sigmund Romberg

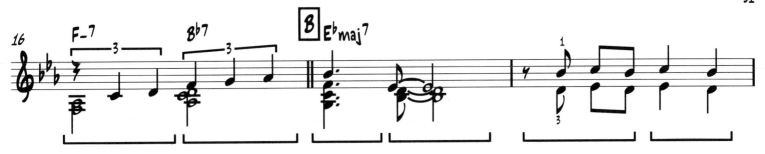

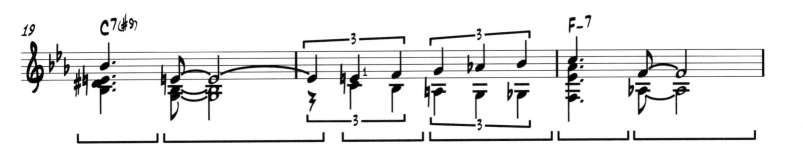

# Star Eyes

Words by Don Raye
Music by Gene De Paul

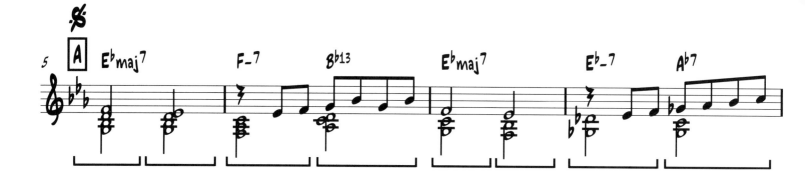

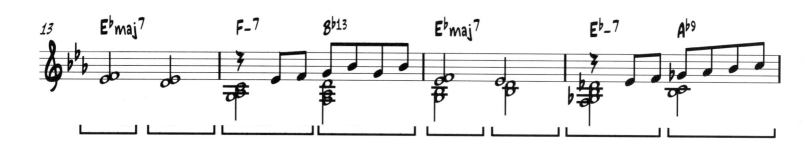

# Stolen Moments

Words and Music by
Oliver Nelson

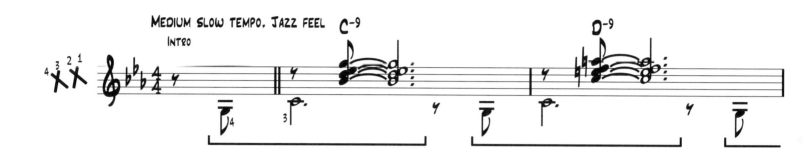

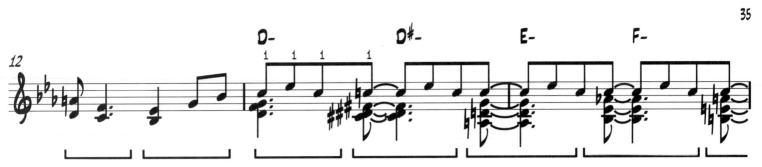

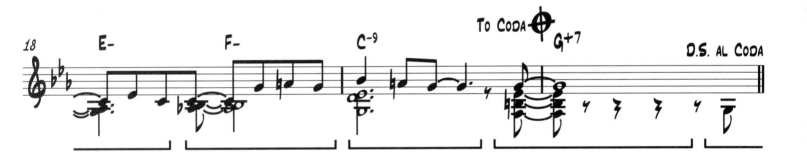

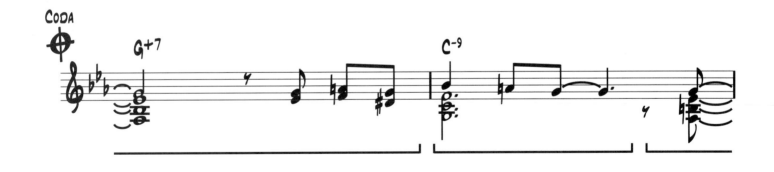

# Take Five

By Paul Desmond

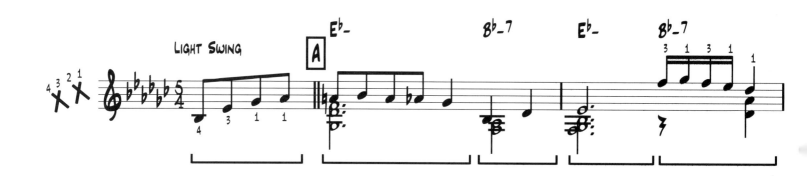

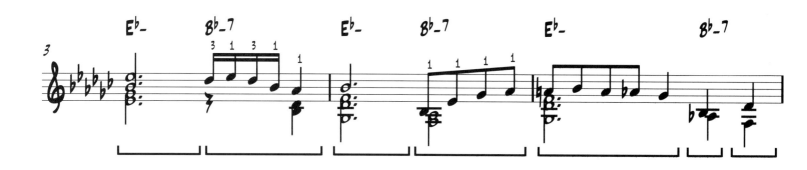

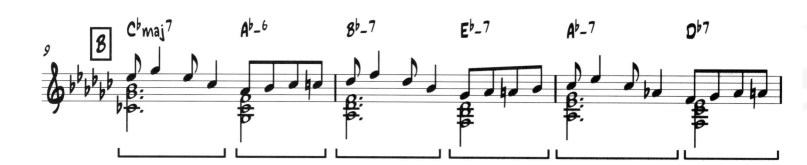

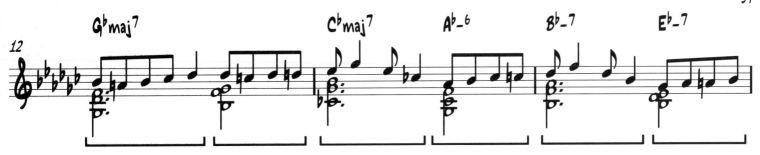

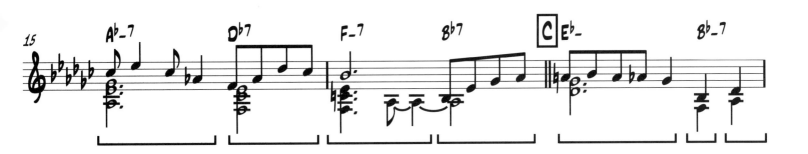

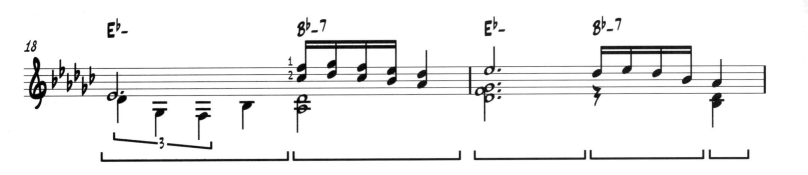

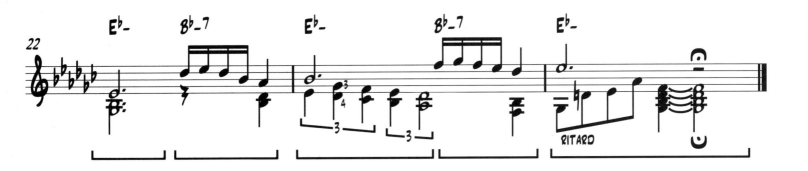

# Waltz for Debby

Lyric by Gene Lees
Music by Bill Evans

# Summertime
## FROM PORGY AND BESS©

Music and Lyrics by George Gershwin,
DuBose and Dorothy Heyward
and Ira Gershwin

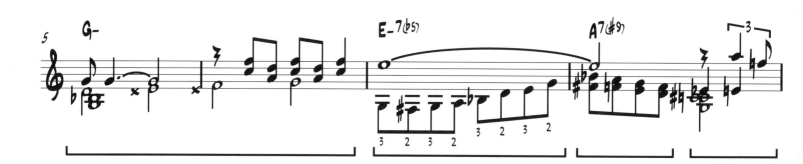

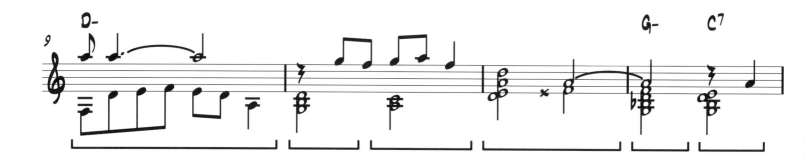

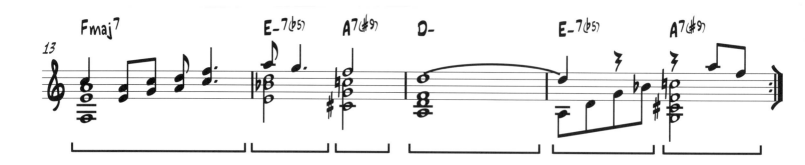